lynne desilva-johnson
the trouble with bartleby c. 2012

the trouble with bartleby print//document
GROUND

ISBN 978-1-946031-15-0

copyright © 2007-2012 by Lynne DeSilva-Johnson
this 2nd edition © 2017

is released under a Creative Commons CC-BY-NC-ND
(Attribution, Non Commercial, No Derivatives) License:

its reproduction is encouraged for those who otherwise could not afford its purchase in the case of academic, personal, and other creative usage from which no profit will accrue. Complete rules and restrictions are available at:
http://creativecommons.org/licenses/by-nc-nd/3.0/

For additional questions regarding reproduction, quotation, or to request a pdf for review, contact **operator@theoperatingsystem.org**

This text was set in Fugitiva, Day Roman, Minion, Phosphate, Franchise, and OCR-A Standard, printed and bound by Spencer Printing, In Honesdale, PA, in the USA. Books from The Operating System are distributed to the trade by SPD, with ePub and POD via Ingram.

THE TROUBLE WITH BARTLEBY *is an imprint of*

the operating system
141 Spencer Street #203
Brooklyn, NY 11205
www.theoperatingsystem.org
operator@theoperatingsystem.org

GROUND

ground, n. : [AS. grund, bottom, earth] 1. The surface of the earth, or the earth as the basis or abode. 2. A region, terri-tory or piece of land resorted to for a particular purpose; as, a hunting ground. 3. Land; estate; esp., in pl., the gardens, lawn, etc., of a homestead. 4. An extent of land; an area or distance; as, to gain ground.

*Existence is beyond the power of words
to define:
terms may be used
but are none of them absolute.
In the beginning of heaven and earth
       there were no words
words came out of the womb of matter
and whether a man dispassionately
sees to the core of life
or passionately sees the surface,
the core and the surface
are essentialy the same
words making them seem different
only to express appearance.
If name be needed, wonder names them
both:
from wonder into wonder
existence opens.*

                                  Lao Tzu

with all the grace of
a burst balloon, loose fast words
stumble off my tongue

CEREBELLAR ATAXIA

temporarily
closed, with an "out to lunch" sign
on the brain's window

behind a creaking
pulldown of heavy eyelid
lurk the ghost verses:

bloated and out of
order, alexia reigns
as they slip like fish

round the corners of
grey tissue, comprehension's
fingers feeble, slow,

unable to catch
even the last word chosen
to be on the team

pulling salt taffy
phrases from the morass strains,
leaves stalagmite straws

on the cortex floor:
a mess of punctuation
and mixed metaphor

GRAMMAR LESSONS

and sometimes "and" creates contraction
like a venn diagram

yes, even when we recall its standard usage
and hold tight to this in our heart's dictionary

(not only "even" but "especially" when.)

in this time -- which is, then,
"especially when,"
our hearts become lazy
and expect of love a synonym:
seek a worD
and not worK
(forgetting the power of letters)

then, ("especially when")

"and" shrivels under the house of forceful expectation,
empty stockings and shoes asunder.

in this place called then ("especially when")
in these times
you and I
are less than either of us apart.

though there's a perspective,
an especially there,
where there's "you" or "I" or "you and I"
(a there where "or" means "as well,")

an "especially there,"
where
it cannot be claimed that my little circle
creates the same beauty as the overlap
of our colors and qualities.

there,
where especially when
the light picks up
my color, or yours, or what we become to-
gether
and introduces the canvas of our days
to this expanded palette:

then,
and there,
may we speak love's grammar
most especially.

TERZA RIMA* and OTHER COMPLEX SCHEMES

To swim then drown amidst a sea of bed:

all covers tangled, limbs sailing adrift

as tortured thoughts came stormy to my head,

with no distraction offering a swift

reprieve - although my work was diligent,

no efforts could these fatigued spirits lift,

no information sane or pertinent

could break the will of the erratic mind.

(Though I suppose it is no accident

that on a day of rest I should go blind

to reason?) Like any bad decision

that rests upon the evidence we find

we neatly plant our proof with precision.

I let the monsters roam freely instead

to take up residence, to cloud vision -

(For maudlin days are to poetry bread;

down this dark path I was knowingly led.)

TRIOLETS and OTHER FORMAL FLOWERS

A museum is full of things:

Of systems built to keep us warm

(In names and clearly labeled wings)

A museum is full of things:

Of categories, maps and kings

(Stories to protect us from harm)

A museum is full of things.

Be wary, child, and take my arm.

terza rima *triolet*

BROCCOLI WITH GARLIC SAUCE, EGG ROLL

Tonight, bad chinese. As hunters seek sustenance simply for survival, asking humbly on the roads leading most directly to their prey for whatever food may appear so here, on Franklin, something suitable, edible, cloudy with a chance of green. Brown rice for the conscience nagging, egg roll for the hedonist calling, beer for...Elijah? No. No. For the putting to bed of this too long day, apart from the pen.

For all those days when silence deafens and you think you will never again be called, that the muse has eloped permanently with another and that perhaps you once and for all deadened your receptors with that last glass of whatever when she comes like a cyclone you want to take off all your clothes and GIVE IN to that inky temptress, ignoring all else.

"Don't go to work," she coos, "I may not be here when you're done, you know..." But you do, you must, you are almost inclined to call in but the economy, the bills, the "responsibilities," you tell yourself as much as she and neither of you is convinced. You leave her though the scent is still on you and you get on that train, writing still, you sit where the students you recognize can't see you just to have those few more minutes and you forget to change to the express and you look up and you're all the way in Harlem and, what, fuck, a hundred and twenty fifth street already and you and your bag and your books and pens falling, and nice job, "oh my god thanks," someone's handing you something because you drop a blank check because you meant, for once, to pay something in a semi timely manner so you stuck one in that poetry anthology and you just make it out the doors, as put together as shrapnel.

I told them, I said -- I said, "writing is like a disease," and I explained how it comes on like a fever, the rush of words, how they clamor to be put out and how sometimes this onslaught is anything but neat, no, messy like a man who comes too fast and it's just everywhere. On the page, uncontrolled, the embarassment of Onan, spilled verse and essay seeds, but of course I don't use this metaphor with them because on occasion I have a shred of remnant manners so I just explain that, you know, it's illegible in those times.

And she said, "Professor, you are like a mad scientist," acting out my sudden shifts of topic and excitability, both titillated and a little worn from this exploded exegesis; and I asked her if she thought I was totally crazy at which point she paused and said, "yes." And then me, "in a good way?" and then she, caught off guard, "...most of the time."

This was after I offered in evidence that night on the roof, when I wrote all those pages about how New York City was a whore to industry, giving herself to the dreams and wants of so many, and how I left this party for hours to do it, and how the next day I knew it was genius because the memory of the ecstacy of words tumbling in exit was still coursing through me but I would not know them, could not read or repeat them. Untethered, like a solo over those four bars, twelve bars, walking bass line which you can voice but never again touch those momentary melodic turns, a gift to the night. I did explain that on that night, too, I was called crazy. Why when there were drinks to be had, dance floors to alight? It doesn't compute, you know, it's no choice. This morning, the haiku:

the drive to write is / most akin to addiction: / itch, followed by rush

What I didn't explain is the thickening and thinning of blood, the tightness of the chest and the sweating, the pacing and the crying and the strange ticks, the talking to yourself, the quickened lungs -- how the words are like a spike like a line like a pill like a bottle of whiskey downed that's still on your breath and in your veins the next morning, how they are more than all of these things alone or together, how unavoidable and undeniable it has its way with appetite and sleep and sex, how it sits like fat Christmas Present, feasting on your gray brain and laughing jovial:

you invited poetry for drinks but it stayed for dinner and is sleeping on your couch now, moved in, its toothbrush staked a flag on the moon of your sink and it shows no sign of leaving. it had to be asked in, this verbal vampire, but now you know it drains you of your blood even as it replaces it with bright red lyrical lushness (when it is so inclined)... the rest of the time you crave, crave, wait and court and you had nails once.

What I didn't explain is that anything but the word, ever, only, is an approximation of this -- when I seek, in desperation, not monologue but conversation -- to relate -- to hear and know the cadence of another's wordless blood in heart beating, to remember a body apart from language layers, as my own homeless heart carries all its goods in a shopping cart of pages, novel overcoats and philosophy sweaters, theory hats and poetry underwear, sometimes as outerwear, you get the visual. But no, more: the essay, the snippet, the aphorism, the quote, the things misremembered, the speeches, the lectures, that conversation I had yesterday: wrapped like cotton candy around the spindle of me, bundled against the tundra, the storm of every day.

I didn't add how sometimes words or hands get through like that one bright beam eluding curtains; the chill on the small of your back as it sneaks out, momentary, between pants and too-short jacket in the winter. The bass that shakes you like a bat, in waves, ignoring earplugs. Even if you make it through you too must be diseased -- either you bore the marks of being thus afflicted and so were ushered in a fellow leper (I saw on you the emperor's ever present layers of intellectual catting, coats of every season, mediated mind), or:

that, Or. or you reminded me, physical, for a minute I was too a body and it was so disconcerting that I stopped.

in my tracks. to meet you there.

I don't know a wordless being anymore, cannot know myself or you without this framework so please, keep it up, both literally (because it's so damn impressive) and also yes, break the trance, stop the flow of words in my head with BODY and say, "hey here is your hand and my hand and your breast and here is my mouth there, and there, and there, and ..." yes. It turns out that I, too, am Biology! if only for a moment:

I didn't say, fuck, how they pitch and fit and rail, the words, urgent like children, tapping on the door of my mind and pinching my toes under these warm morning blankets, go away I asked for you but not ALL the time and then it is too much I want it more than I want you body be damned so I leave you light snores and open mouth to the side pale in first light and slink off to my always companion, this glutton lover who will be here long after you are gone, leaving my sheets cold and stained, smelling faintly of sweat and ill-advised cologne.

I left that part out, too.

CODECI and OTHER NERVOUS SYSTEMS

a aaa aa aaaaa
aa aa aaaa aa aaaaa a
aaaaa aaaaa aa a a a

oeiua aio ui a
ei eoa o ou
uau ioe aeo eee

svrt tl mbnn
xmcjl skkd tnz bbrj
cow word jar
plant candle -
tray, peanut. Water/

playlightrumble
buzzlaughingindecipherablefinger
dripglow

ground, adj. : 1. [only before noun] cut, chopped or crushed into very small pieces or powder; 2. reduced to fine particles by crushing or mincing.

LOLLIPOPS.LOLLIPOPS.LOLLIPOPS.LOLLIPOPS.

2003	bushwick	maine	mexico	streetcorner	forever
your	your	your	your		my
fingers	needles	words	cigarettes		heart
in	on	through	holding	grazing	singed
my	our	these	this	the	only
mornings	hand	tears	stash		lifetime

Into the pillowed coffin
clinging like a barnacle to upstairs
Into this nest I was
flinging
a spent self
with the haphazard toss of done
when
making the sound of hammered coconut
my head and a rafter met inopportune:

                    OUT! like the milk of that wooden orb
                           OUT! my athena, raging
               OUT! steam then boiling, as a radiator bleeds
                OUT! slow then faster, with fist raised

       like an uninvited guest changes the course of the evening
                                    the anger arrives
                                and makes itself known

Did you hear it howl, neighbor?
Did you hear it shriek
Did it shake your bones,
shock you awake from slumber deep?
Or did it come quiet, a sneaking low cry
that gutteral sob a stomach punch
that seeped into your skin
clawed like the sharp edge of damp chill
carried on the wind of this night?

> Did you pull close your coat or covers,
> a wary ward against its scent of sickness
> and melancholy?
> Did your shoulders meet your ears, arched
> like a street cat against the winter of my cry?

with the heart having sent her packing
the brain dissembled, (always of two minds)
allowing residence but keeping hidden deep
the key to her dark chambers --
such a small space for this goddess
wet in fury's juices --
we have lived in strained silence for some time
she and I... the type of silence marked by the timeclock
of a ticking timebomb
so that now explodes
an early easter resurrection of rage.

> CRACK! hiss sizzle
> a bedded breakfast
> of girl and goddess omelette
> but it is I who am consumed:
> leaving no lines between me and myth
> when the howling subsides
> a faint but insistent drumming sounds constant in the temple
> and it is she abed but aquiver, taut
> and ready for battle.

5606: of other years

In the deep of late afternoon, (there is) the weakness / comes.

Outside, though only five o clock (the) darkness (has) descend(s) (ed) like a curtain, definite and black, while the absence of you sits with me (:) (like) a (wistful) silent elder, holding back a century of memories.

Weakness:

for a time that was the name I called you by; less a description of you than to remind myself of my own aching want, and my need to acknowledge, to know it

In the dark of these months, in the hours somehow so much longer filled with the nothingness of cold

I remember you, and the small warm thing of shared laughter on couches left behind, under blankets no one owns, watching shows no one recalls.

It is much more abstract, the want: less a person than a feeling: as though a vessel containing two parts cannot now be filled halfway by either one and yet ignoring Pavlov the attempt keeps being made, each time with less success and more

Sadness. There was a while, when the seasons were fair, when sunlight blinded me against the gaping, when others like gadflies buzzed around me and this noise, insistent, filled the void shaped like we had been. Like a reel spinning when playback has ended the flit flit flit of the film hits against the projector and the imagined life of summertime ends.

The classroom lights, harsh fluorescents, bring us unwilling back to reality: Unforgiving Winter, with her leaves felled turns last year's new growth to brown.

Perhaps it is easiest, as in Ancient times, to personify this dark hour, to understand our own weakness as the distributed sadness of a Season with emotions far greater than we can know.

Could I then write off this longing as somehow related to the seeds of a Pomegranate long ago, and far away, instead of to the remnant nagging of memory?

Patience, that oft-lauded virtue so unfamiliar to me, seems more useful than foreign fruits of mythic proportion, as I remind myself that spring and summer will indeed come and go again, whither the dalliances of the Gods.

{a shaking blech}

I wash my skin of all of y'all.

All of

You all.

All of You, and all of

your traces,

Your places and times all alike:

like the scales of virused verses; dry and angry, hanging on me,

you have left your years and boxes, luggage bags full of dis/ease.

note, please: how

as the selfsame hepa-humour grew within me, satire played:

your thin toxins, bag and vial masked the toxic masquerade

(of the brewing of my bile in those vile, brutal days;)

Rhyme nee reason, true Irony of ironies, these calmed and soothed my aching synapses,

quieted too my own new illness, foie gras baby born of too-frequent falsity,

fatherless inner child of cruel spaces

and empty men.

Lest I succumb to the bilous tide and its acid bath of seeing,

in that nearly-yellowed wood of fear I made haste for Inversion:

opened instead the door, Invited in the smiling devils and began, begot the life in maschera.

Too many, so many nights became mourning:
with the pale light creeping smiles waned and greasepaint melted,

showing true

the grotesque landscape of our folly:

Astrewn in the paltry evidence left behind
the dreams of the toxic imaginary are stripped away, and only a creeping odor remains:

the stink of falsehoods, the stench of vanity, the foul acridity of the game.

Back through the woods of your detritus,
Cartographies of loss and lessons almost learned

paths almost taken burnish bright with footsteps' wear
from moments walked run tiptoed halfway there

I find, journeying,
That new bridges come equipped with matchbooks.

[take care]

without permission
(ignoble lack) his empty
brassy band seizes

this shared hour. my
stranger, your noise precedes you,
has arrived here an

emissary of
insult to the senses, a
sloppy seep unto

your adjacencies:
an ear's momentary peace
within Here's onslaught

now cacophonous,
softness bruised by your office
without permission

We need to talk,
Morning.

You came twice, again, last night; and here I am,
yet unsatisfied.

Uninvited you came, silent like a stalker, and then again, with no hesitation, intent on rousing, you yanked the bedcovers undeterred, inched towards me, for hours: Taking up far more than your share of the bed.

In these linens unbidden, a bad guest and a needy lover,

Eyes weary and cowered, I (gritteethed) wonder if you haven't a farmer or rooster to bother, in these still-dark hours?

Your manners are simply abysmal.

Why, could you not rat-a-tat-tat gently on a piece of furniture when the time came, could you not softly touch my arm? Instead you roil and rage, impatient, annoucing the birth of Tomorrow: a colicky babe, crying for my attention while I am still putting aged Yesterday to rest.

ground, verb: 1. To fix firmly or stably; 2. To place or put on the ground; 3. To throw to the ground in order to stop play.

{just like itself}

for beckett rose

before they took you from your bed inside me, before they
made that exploratory sleuce through exoderm, endoderm, abdomen
before your pale soft skin and hair like a tawny cat's
were presented to me disconcertingly already-clean
and before that same cut would refuse to heal,
reopening as if to remind how unfinished it is, this
business of being born

(if asked,
I would reply that I'm only in my preface, preambling,
while wordless, all wonder, you appear fully written.
do days erase?)

yes. before that.

immediately before, or at least on that day when the pain came
slow and then quicker, a fistful of knives in my gut,
then.
then, when distraction was at such a premium,

I set my hair.

set it just so: big round candypink curlers along the sides
like a layer cake made of hostess confections
or maybe not. maybe just like itself:
dark brown and secretly stick straight serious
now forced to smile in cascading curls
like the hair of my grandmothers
who would have never dreamed of any less
on such an important occasion

{poem for journeying}

in sacred space I
laden yet in light ened with The Work, increasingly
(k)no(w) body:
accumulated explosions
SHA NAno NAno!!!
what a coven of universes, this
what an alchemical plethora, here I
breathe these open faces, I
pillage this silo
of silenced silences
until spent I
leave with mindbelly distended
orgiastic offerings of an afternoon
spirited away, a canteen
for that lonely camel caravan
'cross the landscape of the year

dedicated to the poets of the poetry project marathon, 2012

go on and swagger

let the scent of conquest off

sear them with your sun

EMMAUS

I'm entering my jesus year
and every day is fucking Easter: all
exponential resurrections, all
familial rebirths -

Hark! hear them honking!
three thousand mustachioed wiseman
are come: a transcendent taxicab caravan
beaming bright on the wet dark streets of my
night;

Prayers of radio reverence
waft into open windows, as off hour frank
incense from street corners burns
sweet smoke, plantain and pakora
crumbs falling soundless
like the snows
no longer
native to this climate.

{kundalini}

now
watch

everything you touch turns
to universe
as if by your very presence
atoms
remember themselves
coming to after centuries of
slumber

say what you will of the
light
and the heat, for
in this dragon crested year
man will remember
not only how to build
but how to breathe
fire

vastness infinite and infinitesimal
grain of universal salt and so too a universe,
I to myself sing
OH!
molecular being,
fire neurons, dance unstable cells
even as I rest, here

body bits in constantmotion
symphony of atomic movements,
I am allegro andante al dente.
in absolutestillness,
surrounded by cicada river blue,
I am fluid, I ever exchange and rearrange.

a fleshandblood-bone black hole, I hold together, I:
implode\ explode
and, ahead: the water surface shimmers, titillated by wind:
an excited ionic exaltation. so too my cells shimmy and shake
wind passes gulls call sun warms,
I am nothing and everything
never and now.

GROUND

GROUND is a collection of poems written between 2007 and 2012, mostly in Brooklyn. It was originally produced as a limited analog edition and bound by hand, with its first edition selling out at the 2012 Chapbook Festival in NYC. A second limited edition was made by Dale Pautzke for sale at Woodland Pattern in 2013.

This volume was produced as a collection of existing poems in a range of forms; as the manuscript evolved it became clear that these pieces served three distinct sets of functions or states of being:

1) troubling the site / self relationship
2) sloughing away story, reducing to dust
3) seeking to establish a foundation

During this process, I came to feel that these were all parts of a whole, as well as representative of parts of speech; exploring etymologies, I realized that so too were all three contained in a single, rich wor(l)d: GROUND.

-LDJ

ABOUT THE ARTIST

LYNNE DESILVA-JOHNSON
is a nonbinary queer artist, scholar, curator, educator, and facilitator working in performance, exhibition, and publication in conversation with new media. She is currently a Visiting Assistant Professor at Pratt Institute, and taught at the City College of New York for over a decade.

A seasoned freelance editor and book designer, for years on the team of the critically acclaimed 306090 Books, Lynne is the founder and Managing Editor of The Operating System, (a radical open source arts organization and small press) as well as Libraries Editor at Boog City. She is the author of GROUND, blood atlas, Overview Effect, In Memory of Feasible Grace, Sweet and Low, and Progeny Restoration Corpoation, as well as co-author of A GUN SHOW with Adam Sliwinsk/Sō Percussion, and co-editor of the anthologies RESIST MUCH, OBEY LITTLE : Poems for the Resistance, and In Corpore Sano: Creative Practice and the Challenged Body. For The OS, she has edited and designed nearly 50 books to date, with many more on the way.

Lynne and her work have been featured at a diverse array of venues, including The Dumbo Arts Festival, Naropa University, Artists Space, Bowery Arts and Science, The NYC Poetry Festival, Eyebeam, LaMaMa, Undercurrent Projects, Mellow Pages, The New York Public Library, VON, Launchpad BK, The Poetry Project, Temple University, Industry City Distillery, Happy Lucky No. 1, Howl Happening, Independent Curators International, Hell Phone, WCKR 89.9 FM NY, Unnamable Books, The Sidewalk Cafe, Parkside Lounge, Dixon Place, Poets Settlement, Karpeles Manuscript Library, Holland Tunnel Gallery, the Cooper Union, and in many publications.

A deeply committed futurist, Lynne is always seeking (r)evolutionary possibility, through the building and reshaping of increasingly intelligent systems, institutions, and processes.

For more, see:
http://lynne-desilva-johnson.strikingly.com
http://www.theoperatingsystem.org

ABOUT THE TROUBLE WITH BARTLEBY: A FEW FRANK THOUGHTS ON AGENCY

In 2003, I found myself (a financially strapped visual artist, writer, and increasingly rogue academic) living in a very tiny room in Bushwick (Brooklyn, NY) with no studio/workspace to speak of. I'd already been working with digital art for a few years, and I was teaching myself to code, exploring what the internet had to offer. Wanting an outlet to write and make and share, with no budget, I found Blogspot, and felt at home, in this virtual agora -- a platform offering freedom both creatively and economically, as well as the home for a diverse community of bloggers reaching out across the still somewhat wild internet.

I named the blog *The Trouble With Bartleby* because I felt akin to Melville's scrivener in some ways, in particular the sentiment that I would prefer not to. That is to say: I wished to remain very present in academia and in creative practice, but the m.o. of those worlds increasingly rubbed me the wrong way. I didn't want to play along in order to hopefully be granted intellectual and creative freedom -- I wanted to find and make space for it, and the internet provided that space, as did moving more and more of my creative practice into digital explorations, which didn't require purchase of materials I couldn't afford to buy, or studio space I couldn't afford to rent.

Unless you count the constant "magazines," "menus," and "newspapers" of my childhood, I would say I began crafting artbooks by hand and designing books using a computer (learning an early version of Quark and Adobe PageMaker) around the same time -- in the mid 1990's.

I was never really far from a book project of some sort, and my digital explorations continued to evolve. A 2001 installation, *Urban interMEDIAry*, involved mounting over a dozen multimedia accordion books to the wall with hardware that allowed it to rest opened or closed. A previous installation, *re/presentation*, in 2000, involved projection and mounting of large scale digital composites of text and image in panels and across various media. The pinup posters for my Urban Design graduate school thesis presentation, 5 years later, were narrative, designed to be compiled into the pages of a book. And that's only scratching the surface. More recently, I showed "Perfect Sonnets, by FutureForm™" a conceptual set of posters, projections, sound reels, pamphlets, and other materia for scientifically derived sonnets, branded within the invented future corporation, *FutureForm*, as part of *Books Without Words*, a 3 person show at Undercurrent Projects in the Lower East Side.

In 2012, having become familiar with the world of small presses, press and zine fairs (and handmade chapbooks in particular), I produced two limited edition poetry collections organized around conceptual themes from work spanning around 6 years -- and I called the project *The Trouble With Bartleby*, as this independent production and dissemination of labor felt like a natural extension of what I had by then been exploring on the blog for nearly a decade. The books (*Ground* and *Blood Atlas*) were made using a combination of digital and analog materials and practices, bound and folded by hand. It was the making of these books and the removal of a perceived ceiling they represented that opened the door to the press arm of what would become *The Operating System*.

As The OS grew, I pulled away from producing and distributing my own books via the press or via TTWB, though I made a number of single copy artbook projects and participated in Books Without Words. I became conflicted, not wanting to appear to be building the organization as a "vanity" press. But over the years I've been running The OS, I've continued to conceive of book projects, work on collaborative book projects, and so too I continue to consider both the experiment that is this organization, the books I design, and any text I produce as part of my art practice, not another box called "writing" or "business."

My "art" is scholarship, is digital, is handmade, is entrepreneurship, is bookmaking, is social practice, is typography, is performance, is graphic design, is anthropology, is poetry, is photography, is sound, is fiber art, is curating, is constantly evolving, shifting, is a landscape.

With the decision to relaunch *The Trouble With Bartleby* as an imprint of The OS, the arts organization and press I created out of nothing, I want to say something loud and clear:

> *Wherever there is a community of makers, editors, artists, there is pure potential for production of whatever those individuals, and their collective, can imagine. In the same way that the internet exploded our ability to communicate, virtual access to digital design and print-on-design publication have transformed the publishing landscape. As with any new technology in the hands of millions, this has laid the ground for the best and worst of us, but I refuse to bow to the notion that skilled artists and writers, working together, still need the approval of top-down gatekeepers to validate their practice. That's how the OS was born.*

> *The 20th century capitalist, colonialist model of exhausting, expensive submission and repeated rejection, with hopes at best for publication of work long after it feels fresh and new has long been broken. In many cases, presses and contests with fees survive on the basis OF rejection: very few may win or be accepted, and what funds this is the rejection of other manuscripts. This is a negative model. One that ignores our ability to teach, learn, and collaboratively make, sharing resources and ENCOURAGING each other to improve that work. We will not be made or become great and important off each other's losses.*

And now, I say the same for myself: as a writer, an artist, a scholar, a designer, and an editor, I see no difference between the art I know is DONE and the art-book I know is DONE and the book of text I know is DONE and ready for publication. I wish I knew more about the history of self-publishing beyond the canon, but I can tell you that even the now "classic," "essential" works of Ben Franklin, William Blake, Jane Austen, and Whitman were self published, self funded. The history of the printing press is so too the history of the underground or clandestine press, and radical artists, writers, activists, teachers, and thinkers have been bringing their own words, individually or collectively, to print, to distribution, and to the archive for as long as type has existed. We can talk, too, about the impulse for graffito, with no one's permission, which is much earlier. Whose streets? Our streets. Whose pages? Our pages.

**I invite you: shuck the gatekeeper.
Learn skills in collective. (Or teach yourself!)
Just** *make your work*, **and get it out there.**

ONWARD, Humans.
Be kind to each other.

—Lynne DeSilva-Johnson, September 2017

TITLES IN THE PRINT: DOCUMENT COLLECTION

An Absence So Great and Spontaneous It Is Evidence of Light - Anne Gorrick [2018]
Chlorosis - Michael Flatt and Derrick Mund [2018]
Sussuros a Mi Padre - Erick Sáenz [2018]
Sharing Plastic - Blake Nemec [2018]
The Book of Sounds - Mehdi Navid (trans. Tina Rahimi) [2018]
Abandoners - Lesley Ann Wheeler [2018]
Jazzercise is a Language - Gabriel Ojeda-Sague [2018]
Death is a Festival - Anis Shivani [2018]
Return Trip / Viaje Al Regreso; Dual Language Edition - Israel Dominguez,(trans. Margaret Randall) [2018]
Born Again - Ivy Johnson [2018]
Singing for Nothing - Wally Swist [2018]
One More Revolution - Andrea Mazzariello [2017]
Fugue State Beach - Filip Marinovich [2017]
Lost City Hydrothermal Field - Peter Milne Greiner [2017]
The Book of Everyday Instruction - Chloe Bass [2017]
In Corpore Sano : Creative Practice and the Challenged Body [Anthology, 2017] Lynne DeSilva-Johnson and Jay Besemer, co-editors
Love, Robot - Margaret Rhee[2017]
La Comandante Maya - Rita Valdivia (tr. Margaret Randall) [2017]
The Furies - William Considine [2017]
Nothing Is Wasted - Shabnam Piryaei [2017]
Mary of the Seas - Joanna C. Valente [2017]
Secret-Telling Bones - Jessica Tyner Mehta [2017]
CHAPBOOK SERIES 2017 : INCANTATIONS featuring original cover art by Barbara Byers
sp. - Susan Charkes; Radio Poems - Jeffrey Cyphers Wright; Fixing a Witch/Hexing the Stitch - Jacklyn Janeksela; cosmos a personal voyage by carl sagan ann druyan steven sotor and me - Connie Mae Oliver
Flower World Variations, Expanded Edition/Reissue - Jerome Rothenberg and Harold Cohen [2017]
Island - Tom Haviv [2017]
What the Werewolf Told Them / Lo Que Les Dijo El Licantropo - Chely Lima (trans. Margaret Randall) [2017]
The Color She Gave Gravity - Stephanie Heit [2017]
The Science of Things Familiar - Johnny Damm [Graphic Hybrid, 2017]
agon - Judith Goldman [2017]
To Have Been There Then / Estar Alli Entonces - Gregory Randall (trans. Margaret Randall) [2017]

Instructions Within - Ashraf Fayadh [2016]
Arabic-English dual language edition; Mona Kareem, translator
Let it Die Hungry - Caits Meissner [2016]
A GUN SHOW - Adam Sliwinski and Lynne DeSilva-Johnson;
So Percussion in Performance with Ain Gordon and Emily Johnson [2016]
Everybody's Automat [2016] - Mark Gurarie
How to Survive the Coming Collapse of Civilization [2016] - Sparrow
CHAPBOOK SERIES 2016: OF SOUND MIND
*featuring the quilt drawings of Daphne Taylor
Improper Maps - Alex Crowley; While Listening - Alaina Ferris;
Chords - Peter Longofono; Any Seam or Needlework - Stanford Cheung
TEN FOUR - Poems, Translations, Variations [2015] - Jerome Rothenberg,
Ariel Resnikoff, Mikhl Likht (w/ Stephen Ross)
MARILYN [2015] - Amanda Ngoho Reavey

CHAPBOOK SERIES 2015: OF SYSTEMS OF
*featuring original cover art by Emma Steinkraus
Cyclorama - Davy Knittle; The Sensitive Boy Slumber Party Manifesto
- Joseph Cuillier; Neptune Court - Anton Yakovlev; Schema - Anurak Saelow
SAY/MIRROR [2015; 2nd edition 2016] - JP HOWARD
Moons Of Jupiter/Tales From The Schminke Tub [plays, 2014] - Steve Danziger

CHAPBOOK SERIES 2014: BY HAND
Pull, A Ballad - Maryam Parhizkar; Can You See that Sound - Jeff Musillo
Executive Producer Chris Carter - Peter Milne Grenier;
Spooky Action at a Distance - Gregory Crosby;

CHAPBOOK SERIES 2013: WOODBLOCK
*featuring original prints from Kevin William Reed
Strange Coherence - Bill Considine; The Sword of Things - Tony Hoffman;
Talk About Man Proof - Lancelot Runge / John Kropa; An Admission as a Warning
Against the Value of Our Conclusions -Alexis Quinlan

DOC U MENT
/däky ə m ə nt/
First meant "instruction" or "evidence," whether written or not.
noun - a piece of written, printed, or electronic matter that provides information or evidence or that serves as an official record
verb - record (something) in written, photographic, or other form
synonyms - paper - deed - record - writing - act - instrument

[*Middle English, precept, from Old French, from Latin documentum, example, proof, from docre, to teach; see dek- in Indo-European roots.*]

Who is responsible for the manufacture of value?
Based on what supercilious ontology have we landed in a space where we vie against other creative people in vain pursuit of the fleeting credibilities of the scarcity economy, rather than freely collaborating and sharing openly with each other
in ecstatic celebration of MAKING?

While we understand and acknowledge the economic pressures and fear-mongering that threatens to dominate and crush the creative impulse, we also believe that
now more than ever we have the tools to relinquish agency via cooperative means,
fueled by the fires of the Open Source Movement.

Looking out across the invisible vistas of that rhizomatic parallel country
we can begin to see our community beyond constraints,
in the place where intention meets
resilient, proactive, collaborative organization.

Here is a document born of that belief, sown purely of imagination and will.
When we document we assert.
We print to make real, to reify our being there.
When we do so with mindful intention to address our process,
to open our work to others, to create beauty in words in space, to respect and acknowledge
the strength of the page we now hold physical,
a thing in our hand… we remind ourselves that, like Dorothy:
we had the power all along, my dears.

THE PRINT! DOCUMENT SERIES
is a project of
the trouble with bartleby
in collaboration with
the operating system

www.ingramcontent.com/pod-product-compliance
Lightning Source LLC
Chambersburg PA
CBHW031209020426
42333CB00013B/862